What's New About You?

Karen Hostetter

Messianic & Christian Publisher

What's New About You?

Copyright © 2011 by Karen Hostetter

All rights reserved. No part of this book may be reproduced, stored in a retrieval system or transmitted in any way by any means—electronic, mechanical, photocopy, recording or otherwise—without the prior permission of the copyright holder, except as provided by USA copyright law.

Printed in the USA

ISBN 978-0-9847111-0-9

1. Christian life, spiritual growth
2. Christian life, personal growth
3. Christian life, inspiration

Cover butterfly photo copyright © 2011 by Elise Birk

Cover design copyright © 2011 by Cheryl Zehr, Olive Press

Published by
Olive Press Messianic and Christian Publisher
www.olivepresspublisher.org   P.O. Box 163
olivepressbooks@gmail.com   Copenhagen, NY 13626

Our prayer at Olive Press is that we may help make the Word of Adonai fully known, that it spread rapidly and be glorified everywhere. We hope our books help open people's eyes so they will turn from darkness to Light and from the power of the adversary to God and to trust in ישוע Yeshua (Jesus). (From II Thess. 3:1; Col. 1:25; Acts 26:18,15 NRSV *New Revised Standard Version* and CJB *Complete Jewish Bible*) May this book in particular help new believers grow in the Lord..

Messianic & Christian Publisher

All Scripture is taken from the *New King James Version*. Copyright © 1982 by Thomas Nelson, Inc. All rights reserved.

The passages that are given in poetic format in the *New King James Version* are given in prose here. The capital letters indicate the beginning of the new lines.

Others of the passages are parts of longer sentences and thus do not have both beginning and ending quotation marks or begin without capital letters, or do not end in periods, etc. Refer to a Bible to read the complete trains of thought.

TABLE OF CONTENTS

Introduction
The Purpose Of This Booklet   6

Part 1
You Have Made A Decision   9
    Scriptures indicated in this part   13

Part 2
What Is The New Birth?   17

Part 3
What's New About You?   19
* You have a new spirit of love, and the Holy Spirit lives in you   19
* You have a new Father and family   21
* You have a new inheritance   22
* You have a new citizenship in heaven for eternity   23
* You have a new life   25
* There is a new name in the Lamb's Book of Life   26
* You have an intercessor, a mediator, a High Priest who goes between God and you   26
* You have new power and authority   27
* You have new desires   29
* You are an overcomer   31

* You have new possibilities	31
* You hear a new voice	32
* You have new equipment, protection, and coverings	33
* You have a new fragrance	35

Part 4
Where Do I Go From here? 37

1) Fellowship with other believers	37
2) Receive baptism by immersion in water	37
3) Read your Bible	37
4) Receive baptism in the Holy Spirit	37
Books on Holy Spirit baptism (list)	38
5) Spend time in prayer and worship	39
Books on prayer (list)	39
Scriptures indicated in this part	40

Part 5
What About Addictions Or Other Sins I Have? 43
Epilogue 44

What's New

Introduction
The Purpose Of This Booklet

I sensed the Lord telling me to write a booklet for you, the new believer. A personal friend or mentor who is strong in the Lord may help you walk out your daily life as a new believer, but you might not have someone like that to come alongside you. So I trust this booklet will help you understand and grow from the point of your having just received salvation. In each section, I have given Scriptures that verify what I am writing, since the Word of God, the Bible, is the source of truth.

You have made the most important decision to accept Jesus Christ as your Lord and Savior, but perhaps you know little or nothing about being a Christian believer or about the Christian faith, and Christians might be using words that you don't understand. Before you can study what your new life in Christ is, you would benefit from understanding the words that are used to explain to you what is happening in your life. This is done in Part One.

About You?

Secondly, your life is changed by your decision to make Jesus Christ your Savior and Lord. "What Is the New Birth?" is answered in Part Two.

Part Three explains what some of the changes are which the Holy Spirit does in you and how they impact your life.

The New Birth is just the beginning of your life as a "new creation". Part Four explains your next steps in your Christian walk.

Finally, Part Five helps you know how to handle serious temptations due to addictions, etc.

What's New

Part 1

About You?

You Have Made a Decision

You have made a decision to make Jesus Christ the Lord and Savior of your life. You prayed the "sinner's prayer", and now you have a lot of questions. Perhaps you are even doubting what happened to you, thinking that nothing happened—that you were only emotionally moved. Your friends may not understand and may be questioning you in a negative way.

Don't be discouraged. You have made the most important decision of your life. First of all, what happened to you is that your sins were taken away, forgiven and forgotten, and Jesus Christ has entered into your life. This is a spiritual exchange, not an emotional event, although your feelings were probably affected. The extreme release of the heavy load of your sins, no matter how many or how few, may have caused you to express great joy or tears. If your decision is a heart-decision and not just a head-decision, your life is changed. This booklet is designed to help you understand what those changes are. New terms are underlined and explained.

In the Bible, Romans 3:23 tells us that everyone has sinned*, and Romans 6:23 lets us know that what we earn from sin is death, but the gift of God is eternal life (living forever) in Jesus.* You began your eternal life as soon as you asked Jesus Christ to come into your heart. He is the only way to the Father (God) (John 14:6)*. Because God so loved you and me, He gave His only begotten Son, Jesus Christ, so that if we believe in Him we won't perish but will have everlasting life (John 3:16)*.

Jesus bore our sins, sicknesses and diseases, and our anxieties in His body on the cross (Isaiah 53:4, 5; I Peter 2:24)*.

* Read the full Scriptures at the end of this part. pp. 13-15

What's New

His blood shed on the cross at Calvary was the blood sacrifice needed to <u>atone</u> for our sins. <u>Atonement</u>, sometimes called at-one-ment, means to bring together God and sinful man by covering, canceling, and exchanging our sins for His righteousness and restoring God's divine favor and reconciliation.

We receive <u>salvation</u> when we as individuals accept Jesus Christ as our personal Lord and Savior. The words "salvation" and "save" mean: deliver, health, salvation, rescue, safety, defend, make whole, make well, prosperity, victory (Psalms 91:16, Luke 7:50, Matthew 10:22; Mark 16:16; Acts 2:21)*. This is what God does for us! You are included now, too! He delivers us, gives us health, rescues us, provides safety, defends us, prospers us, and leads us to victory.

Jesus Christ <u>redeemed</u> you. He bought you back from spiritual death, like someone paying the ransom for your life. The only way we can come to God is by being redeemed (bought back) by Jesus Christ. Because of His death, you are now as righteous as Jesus Christ Himself. He gave us His righteousness by taking our sins and nailing them to the cross (I Peter 2:24)*. You <u>repented</u>, making a decision that resulted in a change of mind (renouncing old ways), which in turn led you to a change of purpose and action. (Mark 1:15, Acts 3:19)* You were <u>converted</u>, which is an experience in which one definitely decides to believe in Jesus Christ as Savior.

Knowing we are forgiven and free from the burden of our sins and finding out about all that Jesus Christ has done for us is definitely good news. The <u>gospel</u> of Jesus Christ is the Good News! It is the message that says God has provided a way of redemption (see "redeemed" in the previous paragraph)

* Read the full Scriptures at the end of this part. pp. 13-15

About You?

through His Son Jesus Christ and that we are now a part of the kingdom of God. It is what Jesus and His disciples and apostles preached. The books of Matthew, Mark, Luke, and John in the New Testament are also referred to as "The Gospels".

<u>Being born again</u>, <u>the new birth</u>, <u>the second birth</u>, and <u>being reborn</u> are terms used for what happens when you recognize that you are a sinner, believe completely and truly in your heart that God raised Jesus Christ from the dead, and confess that Jesus Christ is your Lord. It's when we believe that Jesus Christ died on the cross to save us from our sins by His blood, and we repent of our sins, turn to God and turn away from our old life of sin. When you did this, you were "born new" into the family of God (Romans 10:9-10)*.

Being <u>born again</u> is NOT: believing in Jesus Christ only in your *mind*, joining a church or having a church membership, doing good things (works), being good more than you are bad, or never killing anyone or committing other crimes. Although these are good rules to abide by, none of them will give you eternal life!

God is life. Death was NOT part of the Creation or part of God's plan. Death is God's enemy and our enemy as well. I Corinthians 15:26 says, "The last enemy that will be destroyed is death."

God had told Adam (the first man God created) that on the day that he ate of the tree of the knowledge of good and evil, he would die. <u>Spiritual death</u>, which means separation from God, came when Adam and Eve disobeyed God and did what God had told them not to do. Man then became a child of the devil and took on Satan's nature.

---

* Read the full Scriptures at the end of this part. pp. 13-15

What's New

Physical death is when your spirit departs from your physical body. At that time, your spirit goes to either hell or heaven, depending on whether or not you believed in Jesus Christ as the Lord and Savior of your life. The second death refers to the unbelievers' spirit bodies being cast into the lake of fire, which is an eternal place (Revelation 20:13-14)*.

The Bible tells us that we all have sinned, and that the result of even one sin is death. Because we have sin in us, we are spiritually dead and cannot stand before God, who is holy. We can't be saved just by moral living and doing good things (works). Therefore, God sent His Son, Jesus Christ, to cleanse and save us.

God baited and trapped the devil by allowing him to kill Jesus Christ. Jesus Christ suffered the judgment of God! Do you understand? That means that your sin has already been judged! Jesus Christ triumphed over Satan, death and hell, and broke the curse on mankind when He rose from the dead, having taken all our sins and wiped them out with His blood. There is nothing that we can do to get rid of our sin, except to receive Jesus Christ as our Lord and Savior. That is the Good News: that Jesus Christ took all our sins in His body and nailed them on the cross. Because He took His blood into heaven and sprinkled it over the altar as the final sacrifice, our sins have been forever forgiven and removed (Hebrews 9:19-28)*.

Although Jesus Christ died and paid the price for each one of us, that only benefits us if we accept and believe in Jesus Christ as our Lord and Savior and what He did for us. Jesus Christ offered Himself for many people who have or will go to hell, either because they didn't know what He did

* Read the full Scriptures at the end of this part. pp. 13-15

About You?

for them, or because they rejected Him. They will hear the words, "... Depart from Me, you cursed, into the everlasting fire prepared for the devil and his angels" (Matthew 25:41).

Did you know that according to Luke 15:10, "... there is joy in the presence of the angels of God over one sinner who repents"? God loves you so much, and Jesus loved His Father so much that He gave His life to save you.

Scriptures Indicated in This Part

Romans 3:23 For all have sinned and fall short of the glory of God.

Romans 6:23 For the wages of sin is death, but the gift of God is eternal life in Christ Jesus our Lord.

John 14:6 Jesus said to him, "I am the way, the truth, and the life. No one comes to the Father except through Me."

John 3:16 For God so loved the world that He gave His only begotten Son, that whoever believes in Him should not perish but have eternal life.

Isaiah 53:4-5 Surely He has borne our griefs And carried our sorrows; Yet we esteemed Him stricken, Smitten by God, and afflicted. 5 But He *was* wounded for our transgressions, He *was* bruised for our iniquities; The chastisement for our peace *was* upon Him, And by His stripes we are healed.

I Peter 2:24 [He] who Himself bore our sins in His own body on the tree, that we, having died to sins, might live for righteousness—by whose stripes you were healed.

What's New

Psalm 91:16 With long life I will satisfy him, and show him My salvation.

Luke 7:50 Then He said to the woman, "Your faith has saved you. Go in peace."

Matthew 10:22 And you will be hated by all for My name's sake. But he who endures to the end will be saved.

Mark 16:16 He who believes and is baptized will be saved; but he who does not believe will be condemned.

Acts 2:21 And it shall come to pass That whoever calls on the name of the LORD Shall be saved.'

Mark 1:15 and saying, "The time is fulfilled, and the kingdom of God is at hand. Repent, and believe in the gospel."

Acts 3:19 Repent therefore and be converted, that your sins may be blotted out, so that times of refreshing may come from the presence of the Lord,

Romans 10:9-10 ... if you confess with your mouth the Lord Jesus and believe in your heart that God has raised Him from the dead, you will be saved. 10 For with the heart one believes unto righteousness, and with the mouth confession is made unto salvation.

I Corinthians 15:26 The last enemy *that* will be destroyed *is* death.

Revelation 20:13-14 The sea gave up the dead who were in it, and Death and Hades delivered up the dead who were in them. And they were judged, each one according to his works. 14 Then Death and Hades were cast into the lake of fire. This is the second death.

About You?

- Hebrews 9:11-14, 22-23a,24,26b-28 But Christ came *as* High Priest of the good things to come, with the greater and more perfect tabernacle not made with hands, that is, not of this creation. 12 Not with the blood of goats and calves, but with His own blood He entered the Most Holy Place once for all, having obtained eternal redemption. 13 For if the blood of bulls and goats and the ashes of a heifer, sprinkling the unclean, sanctifies for the purifying of the flesh, 14 how much more shall the blood of Christ, who through the eternal Spirit offered Himself without spot to God, cleanse your conscience from dead works to serve the living God? ... 22 And according to the law almost all things are purified with blood, and without shedding of blood there is no remission. 23 Therefore ... 24 ... Christ has not entered the holy places made with hands, *which are* copies of the true, but into heaven itself, now to appear in the presence of God for us; ... 26 ... now, once at the end of the ages, He has ... put away sin by the sacrifice of Himself. 27 And as it is appointed for men to die once, but after this the judgment, 28 so Christ was offered once to bear the sins of many. To those who eagerly wait for Him He will appear a second time, apart from sin, for salvation."

- Matthew 25:41 Then He will also say to those on the left hand, 'Depart from Me, you cursed, into the everlasting fire prepared for the devil and his angels:

- Luke 15:10 Likewise, I say to you, there is joy in the presence of the angels of God over one sinner who repents."

What's New

Part 2

About You?

What Is The New Birth?

Jesus taught us that we must be born again. In John 3:3 Jesus told a man, "Most assuredly, I say to you, unless one is born again, he cannot see the kingdom of God." In John 3:7 He again said, "You must be born again."

Being **born again** and the **new birth** are two terms used to mean that you recognize that you are a sinner, without hope, but you confess that Jesus Christ died on the cross to save you from your sin by His blood. You repent of your sins. You completely and truly believe that God raised Jesus Christ from the dead. You turn to God, confessing Jesus Christ as your Lord and Savior. As a result of this heart-decision, you are a new creation, born of heaven. The "old you" is dead, crucified with Christ, and the "new you" is alive. (II Corinthians 5:17 "Therefore, if anyone *is* in Christ, *he is* a new creation; old things have passed away; behold, all things have become new.")

You can't receive salvation by just believing in your mind and confessing with your mouth. You must believe in your **heart** for salvation to be real. Romans 10:9-10 says, "that if you confess with your mouth the Lord Jesus and believe in your heart that God has raised Him [Jesus Christ] from the dead, you will be saved. For with the heart one believes unto righteousness, and with the mouth confession is made unto salvation."

When you receive Jesus' salvation, you are born again. Your sins are forgiven. You have passed from death to life. You are a new creature. You are a child of God.

What's New

Part 3

About You?

What Becomes New About You?

Let's look at what you, as a new creature, are like.

* You have a new spirit of love, and the Holy Spirit lives in you.

It's your spirit that is made new. The outside stays the same until you change it, but it's your spirit that is changed in the new birth. You receive a heart of love, peace, and grace. You are a spirit living in a body and having a soul. When you receive Jesus Christ, He comes to live inside of your body through His Holy Spirit. Your body doesn't change when you are born again, (although your countenance does), and it's up to you to renew your mind (Romans 12:2 below) by studying, learning, and applying the Word of God (the Bible).

Romans 12:1-2 I beseech you therefore, brethren, by the mercies of God, that you present your bodies a living sacrifice, holy, acceptable to God, *which is* your reasonable sacrifice. 2 And do not be conformed to this world, but be transformed by the renewing of your mind, that you may prove what *is* that good and acceptable and perfect will of God.

II Corinthians 5:17 Therefore, if anyone *is* in Christ, *he is* a new creation; old things have passed away; behold, all things have become new.

Ezekiel 36:26-27 I will give you a new heart and put a new spirit within you; I will take the heart of stone out of

What's New

your flesh and give you a heart of flesh. 27 I will put My Spirit within you and cause you to walk in My statutes, and you will keep My judgments and do *them*.

Romans 5:1-2 Therefore, having been justified by faith, we have peace with God through our Lord Jesus Christ, 2 through whom also we have access by faith into this grace in which we stand, and rejoice in hope of the glory of God.

Romans 5:5 Now hope does not disappoint, because the love of God has been poured out in our hearts by the Holy Spirit who was given to us.

Romans 5:8 But God demonstrates His own love toward us, in that while we were still sinners, Christ died for us.

I John 3:16 By this we know love, because He laid down His life for us. And we also ought to lay down *our* lives for the brethren.

I Peter 1:22-23 Since you have purified your souls in obeying the truth through the Spirit in sincere love of the brethren, love one another fervently with a pure heart, 23 having been born again, not of corruptible seed but incorruptible, through the word of God which lives and abides forever,

About You?

*You have a new Father and family.

When you receive Jesus Christ as your Lord and Savior (get saved, born again), you become a member of a new family. It is the family of God, the church, the Body. The Head of the church is Jesus Christ, and God is His Father and our Father. Other believers are your brothers and sisters in the Lord.

John 1:12-13 But as many as received Him, to them He gave the right to become children of God, to those who believe in His name: 13 who were born, not of blood, nor of the will of the flesh, nor of the will of man, but of God.

Acts 2:47 [They continued] praising God and having favor with all the people. And the Lord added to the church daily those who were being saved.

II Corinthians 6:18 *"I will be a Father to you, And you shall be My sons and daughters, Says the LORD Almighty."*

Romans 8:14-16 For as many as are led by the Spirit of God, these are sons of God. 15 For you did not receive the spirit of bondage again to fear, but you received the Spirit of adoption by whom we cry out, "Abba, Father." 16 The Spirit Himself bears witness with our spirit that we are children of God,

Ephesians 1:22-23 And He put all *things* under His feet, and gave Him [Jesus Christ] *to be* head over all *things* to the church, which is His body, the fullness of Him who fills all in all.

What's New

* You have a new inheritance.

Jesus was God's firstborn Son, and you are an heir of God and co-heir with Jesus. You inherit the kingdom of God, eternal life, and the promises of God.

Romans 8:15b-17 ... you received the Spirit of adoption by whom we cry out, "Abba, Father." 16 The Spirit Himself bears witness with our spirit that we are children of God, 17 and if children, then heirs—heirs of God and joint heirs with Christ, if indeed we suffer with *Him*, that we may also be glorified together.

I Peter 1:3-5 Blessed *be* the God and Father of our Lord Jesus Christ, who according to His abundant mercy has begotten us again to a living hope through the resurrection of Jesus Christ from the dead, 4 to an inheritance incorruptible and undefiled and that does not fade away, reserved in heaven for you, 5 who are kept by the power of God through faith for salvation ready to be revealed in the last time.

Matthew 25:34 Then the King will say to those on His right hand, 'Come, you blessed of My Father, inherit the kingdom prepared for you from the foundation of the world:

Hebrews 1:1-2 God ... has in these last days spoken to us by *His* Son, whom He has appointed heir of all things, through whom also He made the worlds;

Galatians 4:7 Therefore you are no longer a slave but a son, and if a son, then an heir of God through Christ.

About You?

* You have a new citizenship in heaven for eternity.

Your choice to believe in Jesus Christ as your Lord and Savior puts your citizenship for eternity in heaven, not hell! Hell is a horrible place beyond description. It is a place of torment—forever! Once a person is there, there is no way out, and the pain of realizing that he or she made the choice to go there by refusing the gospel is unbearable.

You may need to share about hell with someone if the Holy Spirit prompts you to do so. God made hell for Satan and his fallen angels, but those who refuse Jesus Christ are actually choosing to follow Satan, making their own decision to go to hell. (Read the Scriptures about hell at the end of this section.)

Heaven is a place of splendor beyond description. Read each of these Scriptures about heaven and meditate on them.

Scriptures about heaven:

John 14:2 In My Father's house are many mansions; *if it were not so*, I would have told you. I go to prepare a place for you.

Ephesians 2:6-7 And raised *us* up together, and made *us* sit together in the heavenly *places* in Christ Jesus, 7 that in the ages to come He might show the exceeding riches of His grace in *His* kindness toward us in Christ Jesus.

Colossians 1:5 because of the hope which is laid up for you in heaven, of which you heard before in the word of the truth of the gospel,

What's New

Revelation 7:9 After these things I looked, and behold, a great multitude which no one could number, of all nations, tribes, peoples, and tongues, standing before the throne and before the Lamb, clothed with white robes, with palm branches in their hands,

Revelation 21:4 And God will wipe away every tear from their eyes; there shall be no more death, nor sorrow, nor crying. There shall be no more pain, for the former things have passed away."

Revelation 22:3, 5, 14 "And there shall be no more curse, but the throne of God and of the Lamb shall be in it, and His servants shall serve Him. 4 ... 5 "There shall be no night there: They [the redeemed] need no lamp nor light of the sun, for the Lord God gives them light. And they shall reign forever and ever. ... 14 "Blessed *are* those who do His commandments, that they may have the right to the tree of life, and may enter through the gates into the city."

Scriptures about hell:

Matthew 5:22 (end of verse) ... shall be in danger of hell fire.

Mark 9:47b-48 ... to be cast into hell fire— 48 where '*Their worm does not die, and the fire is not quenched.*'

Matthew 25:30 And cast the unprofitable servant into the outer darkness. There will be weeping and gnashing of teeth.'

About You?

Luke 12:5 But I will show you whom you should fear: Fear Him who, after He has killed, has power to cast into hell; yes, I say to you, fear Him!

* You have a new life.

Your eternal life begins when you are born again. Jesus Christ had no death in Him, because He was conceived in Mary by the Holy Spirit, but He took upon Himself our sin nature. He died for us, and His blood sacrifice and resurrection made us alive.

It's God's grace through Jesus Christ that gave you eternal life. There is no other way to the Father and eternal life except through Jesus Christ. No matter how many or how few goods you have accumulated in this life, or how much fame or how many accomplishments you achieve, they will not give you eternal life. All that matters is that you have made Jesus Christ the Savior and Lord of your life! He lives in you.

I Peter 2:24 [He] who Himself bore our sins in His own body on the tree, that we, having died to sins, might live for righteousness—by whose stripes you were healed.

John 3:16 For God so loved the world that He gave His only begotten Son, that whoever believes in Him should not perish but have everlasting life.

II Timothy 1:10 ... our Savior Jesus Christ, who has abolished death and brought life and immortality to light through the gospel,

What's New

* There is a new name in the Lamb's Book of Life.

When you are born again, your name is written in the Lamb's Book of Life. Your name must be there in order for you to enter into heaven.

Luke 10:20 Nevertheless do not rejoice in this, that the spirits are subject to you, but rather rejoice because your names are written in heaven."

Revelation 21:27 But there shall by no means enter it anything that defiles, or causes an abomination or a lie, but only those who are written in the Lamb's Book of Life.

* You have an intercessor, a mediator, a High Priest who goes between God and you.

Both Jesus Christ and the Holy Spirit are interceding for you. This means that they pray on your behalf.

Romans 8:26-27 Likewise the Spirit also helps in our weaknesses. For we do not know what we should pray for as we ought, but the Spirit Himself makes intercession for us with groanings which cannot be uttered. 27 Now He who searches the hearts knows what the mind of the Spirit is, because He makes intercession for the saints according to *the will of God*.

Romans 8:34 ... *It is* Christ who died, and furthermore is also risen, who is even at the right hand of God, who also makes intercession for us.

About You?

I Timothy 2:5 For *there is* one God and one Mediator between God and men, *the* Man Christ Jesus.

Hebrews 7:25 Therefore He is also able to save to the uttermost those who come to God through Him, since He always lives to make intercession for them.

* You have new power and authority.

Jesus Christ did tremendous works and used great power and authority over the natural elements, demons, and physical conditions in people, such as sickness and disease. Christ is the healer and came to give the believer abundant life. He gives us the same power and allows us to use the authority in His name.

As a believer, you are expected to use the authority and power God gave you over Satan and his demons. Your enemy is not other people, but the demonic spirits that are working through people who open themselves up to those evil spirits. As miraculous as Jesus' works were, He says that you will do even greater works. You are Jesus' mouth, hands, and feet on the earth today. You are His ambassador. You are the representative of the King of kings and Lord of lords!

Please note that God has already done all He needed to do for your life. It is up to you to **receive** what He has given and provided. You become victorious as you take, seize, receive what He has freely given and do not allow the enemy (Satan) to lie to you and steal from you what is yours.

Matthew 9:35 Then Jesus went about all the cities and villages, teaching in their synagogues, preaching the gospel of the kingdom, and healing every sickness and every disease among the people.

What's New

John 10:10 The thief does not come except to steal, and to kill, and to destroy. I have come that they may have life, and that they may have *it* more abundantly.

Matthew 28:18-20 ... "All authority has been given to Me in heaven and on earth. 19 Go therefore and make disciples [followers] of all the nations [peoples, unbelievers], baptizing them in the name of the Father and of the Son and of the Holy Spirit, 20 teaching them to observe all things that I have commanded you; and lo, I am with you always, *even* to the end of the age." Amen.

Mark 16:15-18 ... "Go into all the world and preach the gospel to every creature. 16 He who believes and is baptized will be saved; but he who does not believe will be condemned. 17 And these signs will follow those who believe: In My name they will cast out demons; they will speak with new tongues; 18 they will take up serpents; and if they drink anything deadly, it will by no means hurt them; they will lay hands on the sick, and they will recover."

I John 4:4 You are of God, little children, and have overcome them, because He who is in you is greater than he who is in the world.

John 14:12 "Most assuredly, I say to you, he who believes in Me, the works that I do he will do also; and greater *works* than these he will do, because I go to My Father.

About You?

* You have new desires.

Your new desires are to love God, love and serve Jesus Christ, love others, and obey His Word. Because of these and the new desire to have everyone get saved, you may find that your "old" friends don't appreciate you, and you may not have any desire to participate in the same activities you did before.

Don't be surprised if the people you love are not willing to listen to you as you enthusiastically relate what you have experienced in becoming born again. You will probably find that family and friends are "turned-off" and may want to get away from you. Be encouraged! It may be scary to them, and they may not know how to relate to the "new you". Pray for their eyes, ears, and hearts to be opened to the gospel of Jesus Christ and to you as you share about Him. Love them and be patient.

Do you avoid sharing the truth you are learning about Jesus Christ because you might offend someone? ABSOLUTELY NOT! Jesus offended people, especially the religious people, when He preached about the kingdom of God, but being offended is the other person's choice. You will want to share what's happened to you and about God's goodness and grace. In fact, Jesus commanded us to do so. The Good News of Jesus Christ as our Savior and Redeemer is called the gospel. Telling others about Him is a form of preaching. The following verses are called The Great Commission.

Matthew 28:19-20 "Go therefore and make disciples [followers] of all the nations [peoples, unbelievers], baptizing them in the name of the Father and of the Son and of the Holy Spirit, 20 teaching them to observe all things that I have commanded you; ...."

What's New

Mark 16:15 And He [Jesus] said to them [His followers, of which you are now one], "Go into all the world and preach the gospel to every creature.

We are spirits living in bodies of flesh, and we also each have a soul. Before you accepted Jesus Christ as your Lord and Savior, your desires were to satisfy your flesh, but your "new spirit man" will start desiring to do what pleases God (Romans 8:5). Your desires will be God's will for you as you allow Him to fill you with His Holy Spirit. He has a plan for your life that He will reveal to you in steps you can handle.

Romans 8:5-6 For those who live according to the flesh set their minds on the things of the flesh, but those *who live according to the Spirit, the things of the Spirit.* For to be carnally minded *is* death, but to be spiritually minded *is* life and peace.

Jeremiah 29:11-13 For I know the thoughts that I think toward you, says the LORD, thoughts of peace and not of evil, to give you a future and a hope. Then you will call upon Me and go and pray to Me, and I will listen to you. And you will seek Me and find Me, when you search for Me with all your heart.

Psalm 37:23-24 The steps of a *good* man are ordered by the LORD, And He delights in his way. 24 Though he fall, he shall not be utterly cast down; For the LORD upholds *him with* His hand.

About You?

* You are an overcomer.

Read these Scriptures about who you are in Christ.

I John 5:4-5 For whatever is born of God overcomes the world. And this is the victory that has overcome the world—our faith. 5 Who is he who overcomes the world, but he who believes that Jesus is the Son of God?

Romans 8:37 Yet in all these things we are more than conquerors through Him who loved us.

I Corinthians 15:57 But thanks be to God, who gives us the victory through our Lord Jesus Christ.

* You have new possibilities.

You are limited in what you can do in your own strength, wisdom, and abilities, but when you have Jesus Christ in you, you can do more than you can even imagine. Your prayers for yourself and others will do mighty things. Your love will minister life to others. Your sharing the Word of God and the gospel of Jesus Christ will bring freedom and salvation to many people. Allow God to develop gifts and strengths in you by surrendering to Him.

Matthew 19:26 But Jesus looked at them and said to them, "With men this is impossible [to enter the kingdom of God], but with God all things are possible."

Mark 9:23 Jesus said to him, "If you can believe, all things are possible to him who believes."

Philippians 4:13 I can do all things through Christ who strengthens me.

What's New

Matthew 7:7-11 "Ask, and it will be given to you; seek, and you will find; knock, and it will be opened to you. 8 For everyone who asks receives, and he who seeks finds, and to him who knocks it will be opened. 9 Or what man is there among you who, if his son asks for bread, will give him a stone? 10 Or if he asks for a fish, will he give him a serpent? 11 If you then, being evil, know how to give good gifts to your children, how much more will your Father who is in heaven give good things to those who ask Him!

* You hear a new voice.

There are different voices that we can listen to and follow. Of course, there's your own voice. There's the voice of others, the voice of Satan, and now the new voice is that of your Heavenly Father. With continued desire for the truth and hearing God's voice and learning to know the Holy Spirit, you can learn to discern which voice is speaking to you.

John 10:3-5 To him [Jesus Christ] the doorkeeper opens, and the sheep hear his voice; and he calls his own sheep by name and leads them out. 4 And when he brings out his own sheep, he goes before them; and the sheep follow him, for they know his voice. 5 Yet they will by no means follow a stranger, but will flee from him, for they do not know the voice of strangers."

John 10:27-28 My sheep hear My voice, and I know them, and they follow Me. 28 And I give them eternal life, and they shall never perish; neither shall anyone snatch them out of My hand.

About You?

* You have new equipment, protection, and coverings.

When you are born again, you can put on the whole armor of God in order to stand and withstand. If you stay close to the Father (God) and Jesus Christ, you are in a place of safety. Read and study Psalm 91. (The New King James Version prints this passage in poetic form; for space it is in prose form here. The capital letters indicate the beginnings of new lines as a poem.)

Psalm 91:1-16 He who dwells in the secret place of the Most High Shall abide under the shadow of the Almighty. 2 I will say of the LORD, "*He is* my refuge and my fortress; My God, in Him I will trust." 3 Surely He shall deliver you from the snare of the fowler *And* from the perilous pestilence. 4 He shall cover you with His feathers, And under His wings you shall take refuge; His truth *shall be your* shield and buckler. 5 You shall not be afraid of the terror by night, *Nor* of the arrow *that* flies by day, 6 *Nor* of the pestilence *that* walks in darkness, *Nor* of the destruction *that* lays waste at noonday. 7 A thousand may fall at your side, And ten thousand at your right hand; *But* it shall not come near you. 8 Only with your eyes shall you look, And see the reward of the wicked. 9 Because you have made the LORD, *who is* my refuge, *Even* the Most High, your dwelling place, 10 No evil shall befall you, Nor shall any plague come near your dwelling; 11 For He shall give His angels charge over you, To keep you in all your ways. 12 In *their* hands they shall bear you up, Lest you dash your foot against a stone. 13 You shall tread upon the lion and the cobra, The young lion and the

What's New

serpent you shall trample underfoot. 14 "Because he has set his love upon Me, therefore I will deliver him; I will set him on high, because he has known My name. 15 He shall call upon Me, and I will answer him; I *will be* with him in trouble; I will deliver him and honor him. 16 With long life I will satisfy him, And show him My salvation."

Notice all the action words in this Ephesians text.

Ephesians 6:10-18 Finally, my brethren, be strong in the Lord and in the power of His might. 11 Put on the whole armor of God, that you may be able to stand against the wiles of the devil. 12 For we do not wrestle against flesh and blood, but against principalities, against powers, against the rulers of the darkness of this age, against spiritual *hosts* of wickedness in the heavenly *places*. 13 Therefore take up the whole armor of God, that you may be able to withstand in the evil day, and having done all, to stand. 14 Stand therefore, having girded your waist with truth, having put on the breastplate of righteousness, 15 and having shod your feet with the preparation of the gospel of peace; 16 above all, taking the shield of faith with which you will be able to quench all the fiery darts of the wicked one. 17 And take the helmet of salvation, and the sword of the Spirit, which is the word of God; 18 praying always with all prayer and supplication in the Spirit, being watchful to this end with all perseverance and supplication for all the saints—

About You?

* You have a new fragrance.

Did you know that you are the fragrance of Christ? A person who shares the message of Jesus Christ and who demonstrates His love releases a fragrance. The sinner, who chooses death by refusing to accept Him, does not like the knowledge of Christ's sacrifice nor your fragrance.

Those people who reject you, because you exude the aroma, the light, and the Spirit of Jesus Christ, are really rejecting Christ in you. Don't allow yourself to be offended by this rejection, because it is Jesus Christ whom that person is rejecting, not you personally. Walk in love and grace and pray for that person's heart to be changed. Remember, God loves them and is working in them, even when they don't love Him.

II Corinthians 2:14-16 Now thanks *be* to God who always leads us in triumph in Christ, and through us diffuses the fragrance of His knowledge in every place. 15 For we are to God the fragrance of Christ among those who are being saved and among those who are perishing. 16 To the one *we are* the aroma of death *leading* to death, and to the other the aroma of life *leading* to life. ...

What's New

Part 4

About You?

Where Do I Go From Here?

1) **Fellowship with other believers.** It is important that you **get connected in a Spirit-filled, Bible-believing church.** Do not be quick to join as a member until you've had enough time to thoroughly check out the leadership and get a feel for whether or not you fit into that fellowship. You will want to become involved in the body of believers with which you connect.

2) **Receive baptism by immersion in water.** In Mark 16:16 Jesus says that whoever believes and is baptized will be saved.* A pastor should be willing to perform **water baptism** (being baptized by immersion), if he knows of your confession of faith. It is an identification with Christ in death, burial, and resurrection (Romans 6:4)*, and in some churches is considered the convert's initiation into the Christian community.

3) **Read your Bible.** The Bible is your guidebook, hymn-book, prayer-book, and your plan-book. It is the Word of God. It was written over thousands of years by men who were God-inspired. It is your power source. Jesus is the Word of God in living form (John 1:1,14)*, and the Bible is the Word of God in written form. **Reading your Bible daily** will keep you closer to the Lord and help you know His will for yourself.

4) **Receive baptism in the Holy Spirit.** When Jesus ascended into heaven after the resurrection, He sent His Holy Spirit, which is the Spirit of God living in us. God speaks to us through His Holy Spirit

---

* Read the full Scriptures at the end of this part. pp. 40-41

What's New

as well as through His Word. After salvation, you can and should ask God to baptize you in His Holy Spirit (also called being filled with the Holy Spirit) (Acts 2:1-4)*. Speaking in tongues (praying to God in a heavenly language) is one evidence of being baptized in His Spirit (Acts 19:5-6; and 10:44-46)*. Being filled with the Holy Spirit brings more power into your life to witness (Acts 1:8; and 4:31)* and to overcome temptation. It enables you to pray in a heavenly language which God understands and Satan doesn't (I Corinthians 14:2)*. It brings revelation to the written Word and prepares you to grow spiritually (I Corinthians 14:4)*. When you are absolutely sure you want this, you can receive this by asking the Holy Spirit or by the laying on of hands. You can also receive the gifts of the Spirit, which are used for ministering to others.

Suggested books about Holy Spirit baptism:

To understand being **baptized in the Holy Spirit**, speaking in tongues, and having hands laid on you, here is a suggested reading list:

Seven Vital Steps to Receiving the Holy Spirit by Kenneth E. Hagin

Baptism in the Holy Spirit by Kenneth E. Hagin

Bible Way to Receive the Holy Spirit by Kenneth E. Hagin

The Baptism of the Holy Spirit by R. A. Torrey

Water, Wind, and Fire: Understanding the New Birth and the Baptism of the Holy Spirit by Mac Hammond

* Read the full Scriptures at the end of this part. pp. 40-41

About You?

5) **Spend time in prayer and worship.** You have the honor of speaking and listening to the Creator of the universe. You can come boldly into God's throne room and obtain mercy and grace (Hebrews 4:16)*. God not only hears and answers your prayers, He wants to fellowship with you. He loves you! Spend time **praising and worshiping Him** in song **and prayer,** ask Him questions, petition Him for help for yourself and others, and then listen as He speaks to you. **Pray** in the Holy Spirit (in tongues) wherever and whenever.

Suggested books about prayer:

Prayer—Your Foundation for Success by Kenneth Copeland

Prevailing Prayer to Peace by Kenneth E. Hagin

Prayer Secrets by Kenneth E. Hagin

---

* Read the full Scriptures at the end of this part. pp. 40-41

What's New

Scriptures Indicated In This Part

Mark 16:16 He who believes and is baptized will be saved; but he who does not believe will be condemned.

Romans 6:4 Therefore we were buried with Him through baptism into death, that just as Christ was raised from the dead by the glory of the Father, even so we also should walk in newness of life.

John 1:1,14 In the beginning was the Word, and the Word was with God, and the Word was God. 2 ... 14 And the Word became flesh and dwelt among us, and we beheld His glory, the glory as of the only begotten of the Father, full of grace and truth.

Acts 2:1-4 When the Day of Pentecost had fully come, they were all with one accord in one place. 2 And suddenly there came a sound from heaven, as of a rushing mighty wind, and it filled the whole house where they were sitting. 3 Then there appeared to them divided tongues, as of fire, and *one* sat upon each of them. 4 And they were all filled with the Holy Spirit and began to speak with other tongues, as the Spirit gave them utterance.

Acts 19:5-6 When they heard *this*, they were baptized in the name of the Lord Jesus. 6 And when Paul had laid hands on them, the Holy Spirit came upon them, and they spoke with tongues and prophesied.

About You?

Acts 10:44-46 While Peter was still speaking these words, the Holy Spirit fell upon all those who heard the word. 45 And those of the circumcision who believed were astonished, as many as came with Peter, because the gift of the Holy Spirit had been poured out on the Gentiles also. 46 For they heard them speak with tongues and magnify God. ...

Acts 1:8 But you shall receive power when the Holy Spirit has come upon you; and you shall be witnesses to Me in Jerusalem, and in all Judea and Samaria, and to the end of the earth."

Acts 4:31 And when they had prayed, the place where they were assembled together was shaken; and they were all filled with the Holy Spirit, and they spoke the word of God with boldness.

I Corinthians 14:2 For he who speaks in a tongue does not speak to men but to God, for no one understands *him*; however, in the spirit he speaks mysteries.

I Corinthians 14:4 He who speaks in a tongue edifies himself, but he who prophesies edifies the church.

Hebrews 4:16 Let us therefore come boldly to the throne of grace, that we may obtain mercy and find grace to help in time of need.

What's New

Part 5

About You?

What About Addictions or Other Sins I Have?

At your new birth the "old man", the sinful man died, and the new man was born. God has forgiven and forgotten all your previous sins. Surrendering your life completely to Jesus speeds the process of death to self. Sometimes addictions disappear miraculously after a powerful conversion experience (surrendering your life to Jesus Christ). For you it may be a gradual surrendering to God, giving yourself totally to Him and depending on Him to remove the old desires and then depending on Jesus Christ to help you resist the temptations. Or you may need to be **delivered** from demonic strongholds that keep you tied to alcohol, nicotine, drug, and sexual addictions. You may need to seek help from believers who are trained and knowledgeable in deliverance ministry.

The Holy Spirit is your source of power. The name of Jesus Christ and your position as a child of God give you the authority over sin and demons. Agreeing with God and speaking His Word and rebuking Satan and his lies will make the devil flee. (James 4:6-7 "But He gives more grace. Therefore He says: 'God resists the proud, but gives grace to the humble.' 7 Therefore submit to God. Resist the devil and he will flee from you.") Go back over what happened to you when you were born again (pp. 17 and 27), and you'll see the overcoming power that is in salvation. Speak the Word when Satan torments you and keeps repeating, like an iPod, past mistakes and sins. Tell him "In Jesus' name" to "Shut up" and get away from you. And don't feel condemned if he keeps coming back. Stand strong, and don't give in to him. Remember Satan's goal is to get you to agree with him so he can kill you, but the old "you" is already dead, and he can't kill you spiritually if you belong to Jesus Christ, and you keep resisting Satan!

Epilogue

There is so much to say about the new birth and the life of a new believer. I kept wanting to write more on each topic, but the purpose of this booklet is to introduce you to this new life, not to take you from beginning to end.

I went to the altar to receive Jesus Christ as my Savior when I was ten in a "Decision Day Sunday" service. I didn't feel any different at that time, but I was raised in the church. I know now that I had more religion than relationship with the Lord. As a teenager, my religion didn't help, even though I cried out to God and Jesus. I didn't understand my authority, and I'm not even sure I was "saved" at that time.

When did I know I was "saved"? When I was in my late thirties, a friend and co-worker ministered to me, even though her life was less than spotless in my eyes. I became hungry for the Lord, and through some rough times, my husband and I received help from a Spirit-filled Christian counselor. Through him and a strong church with which we later became connected, we were baptized with the Holy Spirit. One of the first services we attended, I, as a very skeptical, cynical person, received a healing. At another of the very first services at that Spirit-filled church, I remember thinking, "Why would anyone want to speak in tongues?" You guessed it. That day the pastor was preaching on the baptism of the Holy Spirit. In a matter of minutes, the Holy Spirit convicted me of my need for the baptism of the Holy Spirit in my life, and I could not wait for the invitation to receive the impartation of it.

About You?

I never heard anyone speak in tongues, and I had never seen or known of anyone "falling under the power of the Spirit", but that morning I experienced both for myself. That infilling of the Spirit changed my life. At that moment, there is no way anyone could convince me I was not "saved". I KNEW I was, and I know I am! I was able to learn large passages of Scripture, pray in tongues, and understand Scripture that had no meaning to me before. I cried through church services for almost two years knowing how much God loved me, accepted me, and forgave me.

What you do with your decision will determine where you go from here. Please decide to allow God to take you from glory to glory, to develop you into the person He has planned for you to be. The world will try to pull you back into it, and it is easier to do that, but the cost is too high. As Roy Hicks, a well-known pastor, often said, "Sin will take me farther than I want to go, keep me longer than I want to stay, and cost me more than I could possibly pay...." Go on with Jesus Christ and find out what steps you are to take to fulfill the plan that He has for your life. It will be the best life you could ever have!

www.ingramcontent.com/pod-product-compliance
Lightning Source LLC
Chambersburg PA
CBHW061346040426
42444CB00011B/3118